MW01492706

A REBEL

IN PICKETT'S CHARGE
AT GETTYSBURG

BY JOHN H. LEWIS

Ex-Lieutenant, Confederacy

1895

Contents

PREFACE

The author of this little book does not claim to scholar, nor must the reader expect to find any great de of scholarship, but it is only the plain statements of act experiences and facts as he saw them, described in hi-way. Naturally, after the lapse of years, memory is slightly at fault in many things, but the incident facts in this book were so indelibly impressed on the mind of the writer that the errors are few, if any, and the opinions of the author in this book must be considered by the reader, and taken for what they are worth. Without their apology I submit to my comrades and the public my Recollections.

CHAPTER I

In the spring of 1860 the writer of this little book was in the city of Savannah, State of Georgia. There had been unrest in the South for a number of years, but since the John Brown raid [at Harper's Ferry] the year before it had somewhat increased, until now it had culminated in talk of separation, and even war. In April of this year the Democratic convention met at Charleston, South Carolina, and had dissolved in discord, which caused things in political circles to assume a very threatening outlook, for unless the Democratic party both North and South united there was a possibility—in fact, a great probability—that the Abolitionists, or Black Republican party, as it was then called, would elect the President; and that event to the people of the extreme South seemed to mean separation, or perhaps war, as in all this talk of separation there was always linked with it a possibility of war.

This subject continued to be discussed everywhere, and finally in June the Black Republican party met in Chicago, Illinois, and made its nominations for President and Vice-President, Lincoln and Hamlin. On the receipt of this news the people of the South became more earnest in their talk, and did not hesitate to openly talk of secession and war. They even at this early date commenced to form clubs for war purposes. Thus things went on, and the bitterness grew as the time for the election approached. I being a Virginian by birth and a Southerner by education naturally sided with the South, and opposed the Republican party; but not being quite as hotheaded as the extreme Southerners, I looked on the situation with more coolness than they.

In the early days, or in fact from June to November, as I said, the talk of war increased. It was thought by the people of the North that only slave owners were engaged in this war talk. This was an error; the major portion of the people of the city of Savannah, and I think of all the extreme Southern States, were, or seemed to be from my observation, generally united on the subject. It was not a question of slaves or of dollars and cents; but among intelligent citizens of all classes it was principle and right, as they understood it. As I said, being a Virginian I was not quite as hotheaded as the people of this city, and I listened to the talk of war with a hope that in some way it would be averted. I was no politician, and did not know how it might be done; it was all hope with me.

The latter part of October I returned to my home in Virginia (Portsmouth), and I found that war and secession was also the general topic there, but not quite to the extent that it was further south. Still the question was never lost sight of, and it grew as time passed. The election came, and the wires flashed through the country the election of Lincoln for President of the United States.

The smoking embers of discord at once broke into a flame, and commenced to burn with fearful ferocity. As had been surmised, the people of the States of South Carolina, Georgia, Texas, Louisiana, Florida, and Alabama openly asserted that they would not submit to the rule of the Black Republican party, and would secede from the Government of the United States.

While there were but few out-and-out Secessionists at this time in Virginia, 90 per cent of the Virginians were in sympathy with their sister States of the South, and while they hoped there would be no war, and were in favor of using all honorable means to avert such a calamity, yet Virginia, with all of the border States, deep down in their "heart of hearts," had fully determined that if the Southern States did secede, that no troops should cross their border to coerce them into submission.

As early as December 20 South Carolina had formally seceded from the United States, and the States of Georgia, Texas, Louisiana, Florida, and Alabama had followed her in quick succession. Time passed on, and the early spring of 1861 found the country in great unrest and excitement. In the month of March there were differences of opinion in the border States as to the action they would take, but I was of the opinion that, when all honorable means of settlement had been exhausted, that the border States would take sides with the South. It could not well be otherwise; and so it proved. Time passed with this continual excitement; Virginia had elected members to a convention to meet in Richmond in April, to decide the course Virginia would take. It was rather of a Union complexion, but while in session events took place that altered the entire situation, and on the 18th of April, 1861, the convention passed the ordinance of secession. The news was flashed over the State, and all differences of opinion disappeared, with few exceptions. And the grand old State bared her bosom for the conflict; she had cast her lot with her sisters of the South. And taking in consideration her former position among the States, and her high and honorable career in the past, there was no doubt that she as a State would remain steadfast to the end.

The people felt that they had exhausted all honorable means to avert the catastrophe; they had stood as mediators between the extremists of the North and South, and there was but one course left; she chose what she believed to be the path of honor and what she believed to be right.

I well remember the receipt of the news and its effect in my town, Portsmouth. Up to that time there had been differences of opinion; but immediately on the seceding of the State the whole population became united, as they had been taught from childhood that while it was a duty to love their country, it was obligatory to love their State and obey her decrees "first, last, and all the time." Believing thus, it is no wonder that when on April 20 the Government called out the Third Virginia Regiment of Volunteers seven hundred men promptly answered the call, and were ready to do battle for the State and the South.

This regiment was assembled at one o'clock on April 20, 1861, and on that night the war commenced in earnest; it is true that Sumter had been fired on and evacuated; but that night, at the Gosport navy-yard, was seen the terrors of what war would be; the yard with all its shipping and buildings, and vast stores of ammunition, went up in flames; and amid the red glare of fire, with the boom of artillery from loaded guns left on the old battle ship *Pennsylvania*, and as the fire reached them were discharged; amid this glare and the passing of the Federal fleet down the river, with shotted guns and ports open for action, bearing on the two cities, that section of Virginia, and the whole State was firmly cemented to the cause of the South; and men who had been opposed to war, and were

4

lukewarm, became hot advocates and rushed to do battle for their State and the cause of the South.

All of the border States soon followed Virginia and the South became united "for weal or woe," and so remained until the final climax at Appomattox. There might have been, and probably was, mismanagement on the part of the civil Government of the Confederate States, but there was no weakness, no shrinking, in her soldiers. From each and every part of the South her sons came forward to the support of her cause, and from Manassas to Appomattox in the East, and from Shiloh to the surrender of Johnson in North Carolina, and beyond the mighty Mississippi, all stood shoulder to shoulder as they had bound themselves in the beginning, and they fell together in the mighty crash, everything gone save honor and the memory of the graves of their comrades. These were left them as a heritage, as a reminder of the heroic struggle, and it becomes the duty of the living to see that the memory of our dead does not suffer, and to teach our children and the youth of our southland their duty to the memories of their ancestors.

In a few days after Virginia joined hands with the Southern States troops began to arrive within her borders from the South, this being tidewater one of the important points they naturally were sent here. And, being myself in this locality, Portsmouth, Virginia, I shall commence my recollections at this point, and give them as I progress from place to place. Remember that these recollections are written from memory, and perhaps dates may vary a little, but in the main will be correct. The statements will be given as they occurred, without drawing on the imagination. In fact, I shall try to make these recollections true to history as regards the incidents therein.

Naturally, all was bustle and hurry; war was new to us. With soldiers arriving and to be provided for, new officers to appoint, such as quartermasters and commissaries, the vast amount of camp equipage and rations, kept everybody on the move, but soon things began to assume shape, and quiet and order were restored. The Virginia troops and all of the material of war captured in the Gosport navy yard remained under the Virginia authorities for a time, about two months; the heavy guns were being shipped to various points south, and distributed to the different batteries in the harbor. Soon we were in condition in and around Norfolk and Portsmouth to resist any fleet that might attempt to enter. The troops as they arrived were placed in camp, and began the routine life of the soldier, drilling, doing guard duty, eating and sleeping; in fact, in a month or so a great many of the soldiers began to look on the matter as a holiday, and few thought they would ever be called on to fight it seemed to the great fear at this time with many of the soldiers that the war would close before they would have the pleasure of killing someone; many of us had in after years worried for fear somebody might kill us.

Thus the days went by, and with the pranks of the boys who were learning all kinds of deviltry, as soldiers in camp generally learn; even then camp hung heavy on all hands; but this was only the beginning. New things and new duties were to come, of which we little dreamed. Great numbers of soldiers had assembled in that vicinity, and were placed first under the command of General Gwynn, but at the time of which I write were under the command of General Huger, of South Carolina. There was possibly 10,000 men in that vicinity, and all seemed to be trying to do as little as they could, and get as much pleasure out of the situation, and all were always ready to draw their rations and pay. I recollect the first pay was paid Virginia troops by the State, and the next pay was by the Confederate States, in new Confederate notes, and the people were paying 20 per cent premium for it as souvenirs. Some of the people who bought at that time had boxes of it at the close of the war one gentleman, a dealer in wood, at that time told me at the close of the war he had about $200,000 of it, and as Congress made no provision for its redemption I suppose he has it yet. But at the time of which I write there were few people who did not believe the war would be over in less than a year, with the independence of the South.

We had quite a long line of coast and considerable back territory to guard in that department, but very little fighting in the first year. One incident took place early in June that varied the monotony for a time. Early in May the company to which I belonged had been posted at Pigs Point, at the mouth of the Nansemond River, and had constructed a battery, mounting several heavy guns. On June 5 the steamer *Harriet Lane* approached within about one and one-fourth miles, and opened fire on us. The battery was in command of Catesby Jones of the Confederate Navy, who afterwards was second officer of the *Merrimac*, the famous iron clad. The men had been drilled by him, and among other accomplishments they were taught to lie down to escape the fire of an enemy, and it was surprising to see them execute this movement. They would fall at a flash, seldom waiting for any command, but sure to obey it promptly when given. The fight went on for about 20 minutes, and the steamer withdrew with several wounded. This little affair was looked upon as quite a battle, and created considerable excitement in that vicinity, and in Norfolk and Portsmouth. As it was only 18 miles from those two cities, the news soon reached them with various shades of truth; many were killed by common report, but as a matter of fact, no one was injured. But as we were soldiers of Portsmouth it was but natural that there would be some uneasiness felt by our friends. While there was no one hurt, I assure you that every man in that company, from the captain to the cook, became heroes in their own estimation, and all of them desired at once to go to town that they might show the people what a hero looked like.

I have often in after years looked back on this event and smiled at the vanity of man, but as I write this memory also goes back to the past and deep feelings of sorrow rise up when I remember many a man, who was present on that occasion, now sleeping in bloody graves on far distant fields, who had become real heroes, and died amid the shock of battle, giving their lives for a cause that they believed to be right and just, and leaving a name and memory behind them that should be cherished and remembered with honor, as should the memories of all the soldiers of the South as long as the sun shines on this Southland of ours. The North has its pension list as a reminder of its glory, but the South has nothing but its honor and its graves, as a reminder of duty done, and may this and all future generations resolve to protect the one and cherish the memory of the other by continuing to scatter flowers on their graves.

I thank God that the rising monuments of lasting granite and marble throughout the South give evidence that the present generation will leave reminders for future generations that we did reverence and honor our dead, and may every old soldier teach his children and the rising youth that they should as a duty to themselves protect the honor and memory of their ancestors.

CHAPTER II

Memory goes back to the days of '61, and when I compare it to the later days of the war I smile at the pomp and splendor of our soldiers of that day; to see the officers with their new regulation coats of glittering gold lace it seemed that our Secretary of War was under the impression that gold lace and splendid uniforms would frighten the Yankees into submission, and close the war. At this time a single officer had more gold lace on the sleeves of his coat than would in after days have designated all the officers of a whole brigade, and I have no doubt that a second lieutenant with his gold lace felt himself or more importance and carried a greater weight of responsibility on his laced arms than did five brigadiers later on in the war.

In this department, to many of the first volunteers at least, then stationed in and around the vicinity of Norfolk and among Huger's command, the life of a soldier was becoming irksome: they were getting tired of camp life and routine duty; the novelty had worn off, and many were looking for soft details and furloughs. At Manassas and around Roanoke Island, on the Carolina coast, things looked a little warrish, and gave hope to some of the men who joined for fighting and glory that possibly there might be some fighting and perchance someone hurt.

While in this state of uncertainty and repose, the news of [Confederate General P.G.T.] Beauregard's great victory at Manassas [or First Bull Run on July 21, 1861] was received, and the soldiers and citizens concluded that the war was really over, and it would be only a matter of dividing the property satisfactorily. Some of our soldiers who wanted to fight were out of sorts and so far forgot their duties as to request to be sent to the seat of war, so that they might have a chance to join in the closing ceremonies. Thus event after event occurred, adding new features to the situation; we soon found out that the battle of Manassas had not closed the war, by a large majority, nor was there any immediate prospect of its close. Nearly a year had passed, and the talk was of reenlistments for three years or the war. This department continued m inactivity, but was soon to be called to active duty. The Federals had been menacing Roanoke Island, on the coast of North Carolina, for some time, and not unexpectedly the news come that they had captured it, and were therefore in rear of our position. Immediately there was hurry and bustle; troops were hurriedly sent to South Mills, North Carolina, to check the advance of Burnside's march inland.

The Third Georgia, the Fourth Georgia, and the First Louisiana were sent forward, and in a few days we received news of a fight between the Third Georgia and some troops commanded by General Reno, of the Federal army. The Federals were checked and retired. On the receipt of this news other bodies of troops, with some artillery, (Grimes' Portsmouth Artillery) were sent forward to their support. Among these troops was the company to which I was attached; we arrived a day too late, or perhaps I would not be writing these recollections. It was at this place that I first saw any dead, killed in action, and I must say that it did not make a very favorable impression on me as to the glories of war; in fact, it had just the opposite effect, and I found myself looking for a bookstore that I might buy a prayer book to fit myself for the situation. Fortunately I am here yet.

While at South Mills I remembered that in the dingy little magistrate's office at this place I was married, but I had no desire that my funeral should be held in the same room. All of the troops centered there seemed to be ready and anxious to get into trouble with somebody; as for me, I felt that I had always been a peaceable man, and could not see why our boys should be so desirous to go hunting around the country in the way they did looking for trouble. Still, I followed them to see what would come of it. My company was attached as a separate company to the First Louisiana, who were a devil-may-care set and with their marching songs and general good humor we soon banished all fear of war and took things as we found them (not chickens). After a few days in this vicinity (where we first learned the real life of a soldier, which I found in after years was but a shallow education, compared to the full course, that wo would learn later) the troops were soon recalled, as new developments were taking place in our department. The authorities had determined to evacuate this section, and as early as May 1, 1862, it was going on. We, of course, did not know it; but about May 8 it became apparent to all that we were to leave this region for a field of more activity and a better chance of getting killed. There was from the two cities and the two counties about 5,000 men, whose homes were in the territory to be evacuated. These 5,000 men left their homes to the mercy of an invading foe, leaving their wives, mothers, sisters, and sweethearts, and in many cases unprovided for. In fact there were numerous cases where the soldier who was retreating from his home know not where his wife and family would get their next meal. All in that retreating army left behind loved ones that perhaps they would never meet again; but the sacrifice was willingly made, and such acts and sacrifices were being done all through the South.

Thus on the 10th day of May, 1862, the soldiers of this department were to become soldiers in fact as well as in name. It so happened that the company to which I belonged was held back to destroy the stores of tobacco, &c., that could not be removed. Thus we were the last troops to leave town, and on this occasion our exit was made amid the fire and smoke of the Gosport Navy-Yard. On the first day of our service the same yard was fired by the Federals to keep it from falling in our hands; and now the thing was reversed, and amid the flames and smoke we retired from the city with the Federals close in our rear.

As an illustration of the Southern soldier showing that they were in earnest and sincere in the belief of the justness of their cause, not for any personal gain, nor for avarice, but they were moved by the most lofty principles, I would say that this company were all citizens of the town of Portsmouth; that they all had mothers, sisters, wives, and sweethearts to leave behind. They had all opportunities to desert their colors and remain at home; and yet out of 95 men there was but one to yield to the temptation. Such was the case throughout the entire South in the first days of the war. And let me add here, that the women of the South, in all eases, looked suffering, trials, and even insult in the face, and bid their husbands, fathers, brothers, and sweethearts go and do their duty to their States, separately and jointly, and in all cases of weakness they crushed back their tears, smothering the rising sobs, and with the heroic fire of the Southern women commanded the weak one to go or lose their respect and love for all future time; and this heroic fire of the women of the South was steadfast during the entire war and burns undimmed today. It is to them that we are indebted for the love of the survivors and the care of the graves of the dead.

On the 10th of May Portsmouth, Norfolk, and the surrounding country occupied by Huger's troops was evacuated, and the troops assembled at Suffolk, Va. During the night the Federals advanced by way of Ocean View and entered Norfolk, the city being surrendered by the mayor. During the night of the 10th Commodore Tatnall, commanding the ironclad *Merrimac*, then known as the *Virginia*, abandoned and destroyed her, and her crew joined Huger's troops at Suffolk, Va.

In this connection I will give my version of this fight of the 8th of March, 1862, between the frigates *Cumberland* and *Congress* and the *Monitor*, as seen by me, being stationed at Pig's Point at the time, about 4 miles from Newport News. I had a very clear view of the engagement on both days; and as there has been claims made by Northern writers, and it seems that the people have generally believed that the *Monitor* gained a victory over the *Merrimac*, I shall give the statement just as it occurred, being, as I said, an eye witness of the affair. On the 8th day of March, 1862, the *Merrimac* was seen from our battery slowly moving down near Craney Island, at the rate of about 7 miles an hour, heading for Newport News, where at that time lay at anchor the frigates *Cumberland*, 24 guns, being the heaviest in the United States Navy at that time, and the *Congress*, 44 guns. The shore was dotted with white tents and numerous batteries. There seemed to be no fear, and the two frigates, as soon as they saw the queer looking monster coming, began to get ready for action, and as soon as the *Merrimac* was within range of their guns they opened on her with solid shot. In the meantime could be seen in the distance coming down the James River the *Patrick Henry* and the James River fleet. The *Merrimac* seemed to pay no attention to the fire directed at her but steamed slowly on, as if nothing was going on. Passing the Congress she deliberately fired her broad, side guns and made direct for the *Cumberland*, lying at anchor about a mile up the river. On approaching her she opened with her bow gun, raking the decks of the *Cumberland* fore and aft, and then steamed directly for her, and forcing her iron prow into her, making a hole sufficiently large to cause the *Cumberland* to fill rapidly. Then slowly backing off she passed on up the river, receiving the broadside of the frigate, with seemingly no hurt to the ironsides. This fire was delivered at very short range. She then turned and gave her attention to the *Congress*. That vessel had in the meantime, seeing the fate of the other vessel, slipped her cable and was trying to make her escape. And here let me pay a just tribute to gallantry. Although an enemy, the officer commanding the *Cumberland* displayed as great a degree of bravery as it would be possible for any man, he must have seen the fate of his vessel, and yet he fought her as she was going under water. All honor to him and his crew. While we regarded him and his crew as an enemy, we knew that these men were American sea men, and in justice we must give them the credit due gallantry wherever displayed.

Before the *Congress* could get out of the way she grounded on the shore, and the *Merrimac* sent shot and shell, raking her decks and doing horrible execution. She soon ran up the white flag in token of surrender. A small tender was sent alongside to take the prisoners of war off. The officers came on board and delivered their swords and requested to be allowed on their honors to relieve and assist their wounded. They were permitted to go, and notwithstanding the flag at her peak, the man on shore fired on the tender and wounded several of the men who were showing mercy to their comrades in arms. Consequently the tender had to return, as they were in musket range of the shore, and several regiments of infantry and several batteries of artillery were firing on them.

The *Congress* had grounded at a shallow point on the water, and the *Merrimac* could not get close to her; but she finally set fire to her with hot shot. In the meantime the *Minnesota* and the *St. Lawrence* were coming up from Old Point to the assistance of their friends. The *Minnesota* grounded about three miles before reaching the *Congress*, but as the water was shallow the *Merrimac* could not get nearer than a mile and a-half. From that distance she sent her shot and shell, doing considerable damage, so much in fact that the commander of the *Minnesota* was about to abandon and destroy her during the night, and if the *Monitor* had not arrived he would perhaps have done so. The tide made it necessary for the *Merrimac* to withdraw and defer her final work for the morrow, and about sundown she steamed for Sewell's Point.

On Sunday, the 9th day of March, at about 9 o'clock, the *Merrimac* came out from Sewell's Point to complete her work of the day before. Approaching the *Minnesota*, something moved out to meet her. It was an odd-looking concern, often compared to a raft with a cheese box on it, but it proved for its size quite formidable. This Ericson *Monitor* had been building in New York as an offset to the *Merrimac*, and had arrived in the Roads on Saturday night, after the close of this days' battle. These two monsters of naval destruction, new to the science of naval war, that would and did revolutionize the navies of the world; the *Monitor* had the advantage of the larger vessel, being of lighter draft, about 9 feet, while the *Merrimac* carried 22 feet of water. She was also shorter, and therefore could be handled quicker than the heavy vessel; the *Monitor* when pressed would run into shoal water, and thereby prevent the *Merrimac* from closing in with her. This running, circling fight continued for several hours without any seeming victory to either vessel; finally the commander of the *Monitor* was blinded-by the concussion of a shot striking the pilot house, and the command devolved on the second officer, and the *Monitor* soon withdrew from the fight, and the *Merrimac* also steamed over to Sewell's Point, and the day's battle closed. The writer of this is of the opinion that had Commodore Buchanan not been disabled on the first day there would have been more loss of life and destruction of property than there was, not that Catesby Jones did not fight well, but his judgment was at fault in not ignoring the *Monitor* (after finding out her qualities) and destroy the wooden vessels. It was evident that these two vessels could not hurt each other to any extent.

The writer of this saw the *Merrimac* in the dock at the Gosport Navy Yard a few days after the fight, and as far as he could see there was very little damage done and she was soon ready to go down again which she did. She steamed over towards Fortress Monroe and offered fight to the *Monitor*, which she refused, and even when the *Merrimac* cut out two schooners under her very nose, she positively refused to make any attempt to prevent her. Thus ended the career of this wonderful engine of war, and the world must give the South credit for constructing, from comparatively nothing, one of the most gigantic engines of destruction up to that date. The nations of the world were set to thinking, and perhaps the great loss of life on that occasion was a blessing in disguise, and saved many thousands of lives and much property, for by the revolution of modem warfare on the sea it perhaps has caused nations to go slow in declaring war.

As I said, the troops of Huger assembled at Suffolk, Va., and from this time on they, who had been in good quarters, with comparative ease and comfort, with plenty to eat, were soon to see some of the real hardships and dangers of war, for in fact the war up to this time had not been felt, and it had really just began. This was the 11th of May, 1862. From this point we proceeded to Petersburg and were organized into regiments and brigades, the whole comprising Huger's division. All of us were well clothed and fairly equipped. Soon we were ordered to Richmond, and on the last day of May, 1862, we were to receive our first baptism of fire.

This was during the Peninsula Campaign led by Union General George Brinton McClellan. Though much beloved by his soldiers, McClellan clashed with Lincoln and Secretary of War, Edwin Stanton. After being twice relieved of command, he later ran against Lincoln in 1864 as the Democratic candidate.—Ed. 2016

It amuses me to-day to look back and see ourselves with our new clothes and hear the soldiers of Manassas and Williamsburg, who were lying on the roadside, and as we passed (as I thought insulting us) by telling us to come out of those clothes, and insinuating that we would be somewhat spattered by the morning; and it was so. We did not have to wait until morning. By night we were as dirty or nearly so as the boys who had insulted us, and began to look like old soldiers. I well remember that march and the approach to the field of battle, which had commenced.

I have often since been asked how a man felt when going into battle or on the eve of it. On this occasion, when I heard the clash of musketry and the roar of the artillery, with the screeching of shell, that I was not quite as anxious as some of the boys seemed to be to get there. We were halted on the road and ordered to load. The boys commenced to tighten their knapsacks and to be all hurry to go; but while I made up my mind to go I was in hopes that the Federals would all go away before I got there. In fact I did not have as much sympathy for these fellows in front perhaps as I should have had, I was willing to pat them on the back at a distance and tell them to go in, but it seemed to me that I would rather be out of range; but I went and found no one there but dead ones, and they were not dangerous. We got in the Federal camp (Casey's) just at sundown, and it was wonderful to see with what energy the boys gathered the spoils of the camp. They would load up with every kind of plunder, but still kept going from tent to tent; finding something that suited them better, they would disgorge to make room for it, and sometimes circle around in the twilight and find the same thing twice. I recollect that I wanted shoes, and had no desire for anything else. I soon found a pair of boots, a little too large, but they would do. In the latter days of the Confederacy they would have been worth about $400. During this time the fighting was going on, but not near us. It soon ceased, and all became quiet, and we slept in Casey's Camp that night. The battle had resulted disastrously for the Federals. Johnson had gained quite a victory; had driven back the left of McClellan's army some 2 miles, but had also met with considerable loss. To me it seemed wonderful how men could approach the Federal lines through the abatis, interwoven as it was, and not all be killed. In fact, after I saw more of war, I wondered how so many got out alive and unhurt. Early Sunday morning, June 1, we were still in Casey's camp, and the boys looking for more plunder. It was about 8 o'clock, I think, when we were ordered forward to take a new position. There seemed to be no thought of Yanks in the front. We had no skirmishers out, and if the Yanks did they fell back quickly; but, be that as it may, we moved up to a country road, about 500 yards, and halted. Our old general had a very powerful voice and could be heard a long distance. He dressed the line; all was still; brought the troops to an order arms; gave the command to fix bayonets, and his next command would have been to stack arms. At that moment Hooker's brigade opened fire, at 60 yards, with 4,000 muskets. (I afterwards learned it was [Joseph] Hooker's troops.) For new troops that was rather a surprise. (For old ones, too, as for that matter.)

I don't know what anyone else thought; but as for me I began to think that the world had come to an end, and that the splinters were coming that way. In fact I was dazed. I could not comprehend how it was that we were there and had not been informed that we were expected to find Yanks; but such was the fact. I don't believe that from the general (who ought to have known) down to the private soldier that anyone thought that there was a Yank within 2 miles (other than dead ones) at this stage of the war, and being new troops I need not tell old soldiers what we did: We got back, of course. We fired some, but not long. After going back about 300 yards we halted (that is, some of us), faced about, and moved to the front again (but not so fast as we came away a few moments before, and there was not so many of us). Some of the boys just at that time seemed to have urgent business in Richmond. It was said of a certain lieutenant, who was going to the rear at a pretty lively gait and his eyes were sticking out so as you might have knocked them off with a stick, when asked by a comrade where he was going in such a hurry, replied that he was going to Richmond to request Jeff Davis to put a stop to that murderous proceeding. It was more than probable that there were many others in that episode that felt just the same way, but kept it to themselves.

All soldiers at one time or another have been put in action under just such circumstances as the above. At that time I felt sore and my pride was wounded at the action of my brigade; but I soon learned that the circumstances made the soldiers, and in no case did the soldiers make the circumstances; but that it was the duty of the officers to see that there was no surprises and thereby gain the confidence of the men, and when that was done the men would fight all right.

While there was not a regiment in the service of the Confederate States but what could boast of its record, there were but few that had not on some occasion lost its head from some cause or force of its surroundings (at this time we know that there never was any better soldiers on the face of the earth than the soldiers of the South, no matter from what State they come; and not only have the people of the South just cause to be proud of their soldierly qualities, their bravery, and endurance, but they were Americans, and the whole united country has an interest in them.)

There was not much fighting on the 1st day of June, only an hour or so in the morning; and quiet settled over the field of blood, the losses on both sides had been a severe. The fighting of the first day had been murderous, and both armies were learning to be veterans; and the day would come when they would meet on greater fields of slaughter.

CHAPTER III

It is true that the battle of Seven Pines, while a success for the Confederates, the victory cost them dear; but it had the effect of demonstrating to McClellan that they were in some strength and thereby giving time that Lee might be fully ready to act. Among the wounded in this battle was the commander, Gen. Joseph E. Johnston. This made a vacant place for the time, and the position was given to Gen. Robert E. Lee, who at that time had not been prominent before the Southern masses, but was known to be a good officer and able engineer. He had resigned from the old Army of the United States to cast his lot with his State. His name was to become from this time one of the best known in history. On June 3d the army fell back to its works near Richmond, and the usual routine of camp life began, which soldiers so much disliked; but to the above duties were added the additional one of dodging bullets and shells, which was to me very distasteful, to say the least. Camp life is tiresome to the soldier; and yet it is not all a blank, as there is always some "all-life" fellow in each company that manages to keep with his pranks both himself and the rest in hot water; and it is well that there are such dispositions. It drives dull care away and makes the life of a soldier endurable.

My division at this time was in camp on the York River Railroad and in range of a Federal battery, which caused us some trouble (that is, dodging). As an illustration, how careless men become in war, this incident is cited. Just to our left was a regiment, and one of its men had picked up a shell, fired from the battery spoken of, that had not exploded. Possibly he wanted it as a souvenir to send home. He passed our company going to his camp. We had seen the effect of them before, and one of the boys advised him that he had best put it down. But this man was one of the class that could not be either taught or advised, and intimated that we had best mind our own business and that he would take care of that shell. It was one of the percussion kind. He passed on with his shell. In about five minutes there was an explosion up his way. "He had monkeyed" with that shell and took himself to "glory," and invited two of his companions to go with him. They went along, how willingly the writer cannot say; but they went, and deprived the Federals of the pleasure of shooting them at some future day.

It was at this camp that Sergeant Murphy, by his emphatic decision of a point in question, distinguished himself. At the battle of Seven Pines we had lost our color-sergeant, and the adjutant of the regiment desired, with the consent of the colonel, to appoint one to fill his place. Our adjutant was one of those impulsive fellows, a good soldier, and earnest in all that he did. Sergeant Murphy was a tall, soldierly looking fellow, and the eyes of the adjutant naturally turned to him as the man, and, approaching him with the colors in his hand, he thrust the staff in the earth, and thus addressed Murphy: "Sergeant Murphy, will you take these colors and carry them to the death." Murphy, recollecting Seven Pines and how the other fellow had been shot, looked at the officer with a kind of wild stare, created by the word death, and replied: "No; I'll be damned if I do." And the adjutant had to look further for a color-sergeant.

For nearly a month the army, then commanded by Gen. Robert E. Lee, enjoyed this life of care and watchfulness. But the time was very near when they would assist in making more history and graves. During this month Lee had been planning to strike a blow that would surprise McClellan and astound the world. He was about to hurl his 80,000 men against the 110,000 men of the Federal Army, and say to them, "Go back, or be slaughtered where you are." Lee in this short month seemed to have learned the qualities of his men, and what they were capable of doing, and had no fear for the final result He believed in them, and taught them to believe in him-He had struck the keynote, had gained the confidence of that army, and he held its love, its respect, and its very life-blood to the end. History does not tell that in any age there ever existed a commander who had the love, the confidence of his men, to the extent that did R. E. Lee. They followed him in blind obedience wherever he led, and cheered him as he passed, even in their death struggles; and Lee loved his men.

It is a fact, in history, that not only Lee's men but generally all soldiers of the Confederate army gave this same confidence to their leaders, and fought with a courage and dash that no soldiers of the world ever surpassed. Jackson who, in the past few months had added new laurels to his name of Stonewall by his dash in the Valley, had driven Banks, Milroy, and Fremont out of the Valley, badly whipped; had also caused the diversion of McDowell's army from Richmond, and was at liberty to obey the command of Lee to come to his assistance at Richmond; and he had been rapidly but quietly approaching for three days. Lee had matured his plans, and on the 25th of June, Jackson having arrived, his troops were put in motion, and in a few hours commenced one of the fiercest and most prolonged battles of modern times. For seven long days that section of country for 30 miles was to be made a scene of blood and carnage. Men were to grapple in their death struggles; to fall and die in each other's embrace. Nothing like it had been seen on this continent. Two hundred thousand American soldiers were to meet in mortal combat (at this time the Federal Army were mostly Americans; the South had few but Americans at any time), each side fully believing that they were right, and on that field they were going (as on many others in after days) to teach the world what American soldier meant.

[On] June 25, Jackson was in motion for the right of the Federal Army—to place himself between them and their supplies. Early in the afternoon the troops were in position and the battle commenced, and amid the smoke and fire, the clash of musketry, and roar of artillery men rushed together like wild beasts, and fell and died unknown, to sink in the swamps of the Chickahominy. The Federal Army fought with desperate courage. They received Lee's men on their bayonets; but they could not stay, with all their courage and the tons of lead and iron missiles, the mad rush of Lee and Jackson; and at night of the 25th of June McClellan saw that his only safety was in flight, and he bent all his energies to this end. History has told of this retreat, and called it "masterly;" and so it was. For seven days it was march and fight, night and day. Death marked every footstep of these two armies. Long lines of wounded were continually-passing to the rear—wounded in all imaginary manner, with legs off, arms off, eyes out, and yet these men, as they passed, cheered their comrades as they advanced to the front. It would be almost impossible to picture the scenes of havoc that was occurring all along this line. The troops of Georgia were beside the men of Texas. The men of North Carolina stood shoulder to shoulder with men of Alabama; while Virginia, Florida, Louisiana, Mississippi, South Carolina stood side by side and mingled their blood together. The dead of each State lay close up to the Federal line. After six days' fighting the climax came at Malvern Hill, a natural fortress held by 50,000 infantry and 100 guns. The scene on that July day was sublime. The rush of Lee's men on Malvern Heights surpassed anything that had been seen on this continent up to this time; Jackson, with [A.P.] Hill, [James] Longstreet, [John] Magruder, and Huger, dashed themselves to pieces against this impregnable fortress, and left their dead within the Federal lines. Such courage as was seen that day equaled Waterloo; but the position was impregnable, and night closed this scene of blood with McClellan still in possession of the hill; but when morning came again he was in full retreat to the James River, and on July 2d he was hemmed in, crippled, and defeated, driven 80 miles, and with a loss of 25,000 of his best troops.

We of the Confederate army had victory and the spoils of war to cheer us: but we also had to mourn the loss of many loved officers and comrades. In fact there was few companies in the vast army but what had lost some loved friend.

About the 6th of July the army of Lee commenced to fall back to their works, near Richmond, to repair and rest for other trials; marches, and battles yet to come. The army lay quiet for several weeks, talking of peace and speculating on the chances of the war being over or near its close. Each soldier thought that the great defeat of the army of the Potomac would end the matter. The great idea was foreign intervention, peace, and home.

One of the constant, terrible anxieties for the Lincoln administration was the possibility that foreign powers would recognize or even aid the Confederacy.—Ed. 2016

Notwithstanding the sadness created by the loss of comrades, we were seemingly joyous, and, like selfish human nature, forgot for the time the sorrow that was caused in the homes of the widows and orphans, both North and South, who would be waiting for the footsteps of those that would never come.

Soldiers are not heathens; but the life of danger seems to cause them soon to forget the past. They take no thought of the future, and nothing but the present lives with them; and they make the most of it.

After such hardships as we had passed through, the quiet of the camp was very acceptable and pleasant. Yet, while we were at rest, the "powers that be" at the heads of the two armies were busy planning complex movements for our amusement. Of course we soldiers knew nothing of this; but we found it out as we went along. It was probably well that we did not know of it at the time or there might have been more of us on the sick list. There are other kinds of sickness that soldiers have beside sea-sickness. Just before a battle weakness in the knees and various other kinds of weakness— sometimes a weakness to want to be anywhere but there.

There was a man by the name of [General John] Pope, not much known to fame, who suddenly burst on the horizon of war. He had, it was said (in fact he said so himself), his headquarters where his hindquarters ought to have been, in the saddle. He also stated confidentially that he was from the West, but did not say how long he was going to stay in that locality. Perhaps he did not know at that time; he was not a well-read man; nor did he consult either [Union Generals Nathaniel] Banks, [Robert] Milroy, or [John C.] Fremont, which, had he have done, perhaps they would have informed him that there were a couple of men who came that way sometimes by the names of R. E. Lee and Stonewall Jackson, who might object to his lying around and cause him serious trouble, and without his consent direct his retirement. Pope soon found this to be the case. Lee seeing that the army of McClellan at Harrison's Landing was paralyzed, concluded to send Jackson to Culpepper Court-House to investigate Pope. Accordingly he gave the order, and the "Man of Destiny" moved forward. He soon found Pope scattered around the country, making war on the defenseless inhabitants of that section. He (Pope) was seemingly teaching a "School for Scandal;" in other words making thieves of his whole army by orders of Major-General

John Pope. Jackson, you know, was a sort of churchman, and he objected to this mode of procedure. His orders were liberal, and allowed him to act at his discretion. Falling in with his old commissary, Banks, Jackson concluded to tell him, and through him Pope, that this mode of plundering the people must stop. He put his army in motion, and the battle of Cedar Mountain was the result. Banks as usual sent that same old story to Pope that he could manage this little affair by himself, as the rebels were in full retreat. This was at 4 o'clock p m., August 8, 1862. Almost before the courier had fairly started with his dispatch Banks and his whole command was after him, and Jackson's men after them both. At sundown Banks was in full retreat through the cornfields, and Jackson had quiet possession of the corn and many other little things, such as artillery, muskets, baggage, and prisoners of war. There was the usual pow-wow. Pope said it was Banks, and Banks said it was Pope. But "it was so, all the same." Jackson quietly withdrew next day, and gave Pope a chance to send dispatches to Washington, as suited the occasion.

In the meantime Lee was coming up with his old veterans. For, be it known that all of his troops could justly be designated as such, it was not long after this that the word ragged was added, making them Lee's ragged veterans, "of whom Lee remarked that he never was ashamed of when fighting." This march is well remembered by the writer. The weather was very hot, the marching and countermarching was rapid, and the troops suffered greatly, many falling by the roadside in utter exhaustion-many perhaps never to be heard of again.

To the old soldiers I need not tell of these hardships and sufferings of the troops; and if it were possible for me to describe it as it was to the rising generation, they would perhaps look on it as a picture of the imagination. But it is for the youth that we of that day should write and relate, that they may learn what the sufferings of the men of that day were and learn the value of a faithful adherence to what they believe, as we believed, to be right. I will not raise the question here, nor do I desire to raise it at all, or to bring any argument in this book to prove one way or the other, but I do not hesitate to say, without any attempt to justify or excuse, that we, the Southern people of that day, did fully believe in the righteousness of our cause; and as proof of this assertion see our 300,000 graves, our thousands of widows and orphans, and at the close of the war our impoverished homes; but even better proof exists than even that. See the survivors, in all honor, submitting quietly to the arbitrament of war, to which they had submitted their cause, teaching their youth to become good citizens of this united country, neither casting or desiring to cast from the close of the war to the present time any impediment to its growth or glory, but by their efforts assisting in both. Let all the people of this vast country look at these facts, and say whether the people of the South were not earnest in their belief that they were right.

Lee having arrived with the balance of his army the game of war commenced between him and Pope. (The army was at this time divided in right and left wings, Jackson commanding the left and Longstreet the right.) It seemed to be the intention of Lee to make this campaign short and sharp. McClellan had been quietly beheaded, and his army was being forwarded to Pope by sea. It was Lee's desire to do Pope up, and retire him before the men from Harrisons Landing should arrive to his support. To this end he gave his energies. About August 5 he conceived the bold plan of sending Jackson to the right and rear of Pope's army—that is, between Pope and Washington—while Longstreet should amuse him in front on the Rappahannock River. Jackson moved by quick marches, passing Manassas, and destroying vast quantities of stores. It was at this point, where vast quantities of sutler's stores were destroyed, that was seen the most novel sight that perhaps was ever seen before in an army. These stores, of course, were intended for the Federal soldiers, and composed all kinds of delicacies. The men of Jackson were told to help themselves, and then were seen men, 6 feet tall, ragged, acting like school boys, with a stick of candy in one hand and a pickle in the other, a laughing, howling, frolicking set, who a few days before had been living on green corn, were feasting on sardines and wine and other delicacies. But time was of the greatest importance, and with sorrow, and their haversacks full, they had to leave much to the flames. Of course the Yankee sutlers lost nothing by this destruction; they simply charged double price to the Yanks until the price was made up.

About the 28th Jackson was well posted, but Pope was between him and his friends, and as usual he telegraphed to Washington that he had Jackson bagged and would soon commence to tie the bag up. He sent orders to his different commanders how to move and when to commence tying the bag.

They moved, and like the Irishman's flea, Jackson was not there.

Longstreet in the meantime was hurrying up by forced marches, night and day; he pressed forward, and ere Pope was aware of it he was deploying on Jackson's right.

History tells how Pope attacked Jackson under the impression that he (Jackson) was in full retreat; how he told the Washington people that the awful bugbear, Stonewall, was gone up: history will also tell you how, on the 30th of August, the bag of Jackson burst asunder, and its fragments were scattered from Manassas to Washington with a pretty good slice on its way to Richmond as prisoners of war. It will also tell that the head of Pope that day fell in the basket along with them that had gone before, and that in two short months the Man of the West, with his headquarters in the saddle, vanished from view and was placed among the things "that might have been." Thus ended the fame and glory of Pope; his name has never been mentioned in that locality since. Thus closed the battle of Manassas and the career of Pope in the Army of the Potomac.

CHAPTER IV

Pope had disappeared from the scene, but still the war went on; it seemed that with every disaster the North grew stronger, but in the present dilemma it was necessary that the powers at Washington should move quick, as the body of McClellan was not quite dead, although it had been beheaded. The powers at Washington, including War, Navy, and even the Fish Commission, called loudly to awaken him, Little Mac, back to life, that he might again place himself at the head of the dispirited Army of the Potomac, and make some effort to stay the victorious march of Lee.

September 3 found Lee and his victorious army on his way to the Potomac with little opposition, with the intention of crossing into "Maryland, My Maryland." His aim seemed to be to read the riot act to the United States Government, and to invite the people of that State to accept the freedom that it was said had been denied them by the Federal authorities. While in Baltimore and eastern Maryland there were thousands who favored the Southern cause, and would have welcomed Lee and his army, yet in this section there were few to respond to Lee's invitation. As an instance of the feeling of the people of Baltimore, I relate one circumstance that occurred to myself. In 1863, I was captured at Gettysburg, Pennsylvania, in the battle of the third day [July 3], in the charge of Pickett's division. I was carried to Baltimore in a box car, with many others; we were delayed just outside the city limits for three or four hours; it was July 5, and the sun was extremely hot. The battle of Gettysburg had just been fought, and my wife being within the Federal lines, I knew that she would get the report, and naturally suffer great anxiety, knowing that I was in the division of Pickett, which had been so badly cut up. Therefore I was desirous of getting word to her as soon as possible, and knowing that Baltimore contained many that sympathized with us, I resolved to make the attempt to get word to her. Standing as near to the cars as the guards would permit were two young ladies, about 20 years of age; they seemed to take great interest in us, and looked sympathetic. I procured a piece of paper and pencil, and wrote on it my name and the address of my wife, requesting that she be informed that her husband was well and unhurt. As the guards were going from me, having rolled the paper up, I threw it at the feet of the young ladies; they seemed to know my desire; and one of them immediately put her foot on it and looked at me, and I knew from the look my wife would hear of me. She dared not pick it up, but with the patience and fortitude of a martyr she stood for over two hours in that July sun, until the train moved off, and in a day or two my wife received an unsigned letter from Baltimore, stating that the writer had seen her husband as a prisoner of war, and he was well. I have blessed that lady from that day, and classed her as near the angels as any mortal ever can get in this world.

There were, as I said, thousands of glorious women and men in Baltimore and eastern Maryland, yet Lee's manifesto of peace and freedom fell flat on the people of western Maryland, and the thousands that we had expected to get dwindled down to perhaps one company. However, we were in Maryland, feeding on green corn. The army of Lee had turned to horses as far as feed went; we had our regular six ears to the man (or horse, as you please—fact).

History records the lost order of Lee,* and how by that means McClellan was enabled to press so closely on Lee. At Frederick, Maryland, the army was divided from its purpose of capturing Harper's Ferry.

*Lee issued Special Order 191 before the Battle of Antietam. A copy of the order was recovered by Union soldiers of the 27th Indiana. The order provided valuable information concerning the Army of Northern Virginia's movements and campaign plans. Upon receiving this information, McClellan exclaimed, "Here is a paper with which, if I cannot whip Bobby Lee, I will be willing to go home."—Ed. 2016

My division, R. H. Anderson's, was with McLaw's command in the Pleasant Valley, and on Maryland Heights, with Jackson on the Virginia side, and Confederates on London Heights. The officer commanding Harper's Ferry made very little resistance, and the place fell with 11,000 prisoners, 73 guns, vast quantities of stores, munitions of war, wagons, etc.

Harper's Ferry changed hands eight times between 1861 and 1865. The Battle of Harpers Ferry referred to here was fought September 12–15, 1862.—Ed. 2016

Then came the race for Sharpsburg, where Lee was with the remnant of his army, and the near approach of the Federal army made it look serious. The racehorse speed of Jackson brought him to Lee on September 16, and somewhat altered things; but Lee, with his depleted army of not more than 25,000 men was far from safe, in the face of 90,000 Federal troops under McClellan, whose head been replaced upon his body for this occasion only.* Poor Mac; your lot was hard. While there were no full generals killed in action on the Federal side, there were numbers of them buried in oblivion; nearly every battle, at the beginning of the war, was sure death to its commander; that is, he was relieved from further service.

After being relieved by Lincoln once, McClellan was restored to command briefly.—Ed. 2016

The battles as the war progressed seemed to increase in violence, and each one was more severe than the preceding one, so at Sharpsburg this rule was followed, and this battle proved to be one of the bloodiest fought up to that time. The odds were fearfully in favor of the Federals, being at some points as many as ten to one, and the average three to one during the entire action. The estimate of Lee's force was taken from the morning report of the 6th, and it is no criterion to judge his strength on the 17th. At that time I was orderly sergeant of Company G, Ninth Virginia Infantry. My report of September 16 showed 40 men for duty. When going into action on the 17th I commanded the company as sergeant, and had only six men. This is easily accounted for. My brigade made a night march from Harper's Ferry, and halted at midnight for one hour; soon an order came urging us forward, but the men had fallen asleep and did not wake; at least two-thirds of the brigade were left in the woods; some will say that these men were shirkers; it was not so; these men were but human, and their endurance had reached its limit. All these men, with few exceptions, were soldiers that could be depended on in any emergency, and they came up as soon as they could.

Lee's army was in better condition on the 18th than it was on the 17th, even allowing for the loss, according to my observation. It is not necessary to go into history as regards this battle; the account is short; Lee, with his army of not more than 30,000 men, repulsed the attacks of McClellan's 90,000 men, held the field until night of the 18th, and then quietly withdrew his force across the river without the loss of a single gun. Early that morning I saw Lee and Jackson in the middle of the Potomac, sitting quietly on their horses, watching the last of their troops pass over.

The Army of Northern Virginia had on these September days added glory to its name, and was more closely cemented together by the blood of its comrades, and if possible had learned to love Lee and Jackson, and their immediate commanders, better than ever.

As of this writing, in 2016, Antietam remains the bloodiest single-day battle in American history, with a combined tally of dead, wounded, and missing at 22,717.—Ed.

There is one incident of this battle that attracted my attention. During the 17th it became necessary to move our brigade by the left flank, and the fire of shot and shell was very heavy and dangerous, Jackson was sitting on his horse just in rear of us. Our general had been wounded, and Colonel Hodges, of the Fourteenth Virginia Regiment, was commanding. We were moving in common time; Jack-son, seeing the danger to which it was exposed, told the colonel to move in double quick time out of danger. This incident only goes to show how thoughtful Jackson was in small things, and how careful he was of his men, when it was possible, and yet when fighting was necessary he was all fire, and life for the time being amounted to very little. With him war meant fight, and fight meant kill, and that was the secret of his success, combined with his race-horse speed of movements, 'The men of our army were as a general rule as true as steel; but there were exceptions, as in the case that I shall relate. When crossing the Potomac, going to the field, one of the men, who was accustomed to being in the rear when a fight was in progress, and at the same time have a plausible excuse for it, was on this occasion, as he said, nearly caught. He had crossed the canal, and to save his shoes had taken them off. He had no idea of a fight at this point; but while washing his feet, preparatory to putting on his shoes, a gun in front gave notice of something wrong going on. He listened intently for further evidence of the situation, and hearing several guns in quick succession he deliberately threw his shoes in the canal, with the expression (alluding to the shoes), you came very near getting me in trouble this time, and retired to the rear, giving as an excuse no shoes. To the reverse of this I have seen on the line of battle men barefooted, with feet bleeding, facing death in all forms of horror, and pleading no excuse to escape from what they felt to be their duty. There is no place better than a field of battle to test the higher qualities and the nobility of man.

My division (R. H. Anderson's) was the rear guard on this occasion, and my regiment was left on the river as a picket line, and we suffered for want of something to eat. Rations were furnished us at Harper's Ferry on the 16th, and not much then.

It was now the 18th, and nothing had been furnished since; nor did we get any until the 19th. I did not eat anything for at least forty-eight hours. You may not possibly know how it feels to go that long, and to be marching night and day; I assure you that a man is not in the best of spirits. Such was the case often in the Confederate army at this date, and in the latter days it was a general thing, with only an occasional exception, to prove the rule.

On the night of the 18th of September, as I said, Lee crossed the river, back to Virginia. When going over the river the boys were singing "Maryland, my Maryland." But all was quiet on that point when we came back. Occasionally some fellow would strike that tune, and you would then hear the echo, "Damn My Maryland." All seemed to be disgusted with that part of Maryland.

The army continued its March to Bunker Hill, near Winchester. Grand old Winchester, who's history in the past stood out in glittering brightness and honor, was by the action of her people, their fortitude, patience, and suffering, to add new glory, if possible, to that history; and to-day their enemies of that day, after cool reflection, and remembering the days of '76, must give them credit for their firm adherence to principles that are truly American and originated in America.

These people of the South were descendants of some of the greatest heroes and most learned men of our country. The blood of the heroes of the Alamo, "who had no messenger of defeat," flowed through their veins, and while in the heat of passion, while blinded by political dissensions and demagogism, there was some excuse for condemnation. Today there should be nothing but praise when we hold up as examples of American manhood the soldiers of both North and South as an illustration to the world of what America is, and the South, with the North, should at least share some of the glory attached to the name of America.

Let the North and the South have their own private opinions as to past days; but let the soldiers of both armies now living resolve that they will not themselves, nor will they permit politicians to, make capital for themselves by causing discord between the men of both armies, who, by their heroism, the dauntless bravery of the living, and the graves of the dead, have taught the world to keep their hands off American affairs.

Here at Bunker Hill we rested for some time from marches and battles. Cold weather was approaching, and many of the men were poorly clad and numbers without shoes; but we were getting used to that damp life is not good for soldiers. It gives him time to think of home, and in our case sad thoughts would arise when we looked back to home and loved ones, and knew, while our sufferings were great to feel, that those we loved were, perchance, suffering more than we.

It is true that the Southern women sent cheerful messages to camp when in many cases their hearts were filled with sadness. It is no wonder that the women of the South of that day were looked on as very near the angels by all of the Southern soldiers.

It was at this camp that my first attempt was made as a poet. I shall ever recollect that night of November, with the howling blast of early winter passing through the trees, with men sleeping around on the bare earth, with nothing to shelter them or to cover with. There, sitting over a smoking fire, with thoughts of home, and, rubbing my eyes, smarting from the smoke of the fire, I have often, in after years, in thinking of that night, wondered how it was even possible for my thoughts to run in a poetical channel; but they did, and [a poem flowed] produced on brown paper and by the light of the fire. It has not been altered in any manner.

We soon fitted a tune to these lines and sung them at our camp-fires at night to drive dull care away. The reader may judge from the last few lines of this poetical "delusion" that the writer at that time thought that things looked bright for peace. In fact it was while at this camp that various rumors of recognition by France, England, and other powers began to look to us as truth, and such talk would send our spirits up, only to fall again. But up to this time there was really no despondency among the men in the army. There were some few that were always croaking, but not a great many.

About this time I met a man from my town that I had not seen for years, and his words were prophetic. He was in a Texas regiment, and he having left home several years prior to the war I was glad to meet him, and among other things I asked him what he thought of the war. He said that it was his opinion that in two years we would be down on the "Gulf of Mexico, with the seat of our pants out (mine were out then), fishing for our breakfast with a pin-hook." I said, "I guess not;" but he was near right; for in about two years many of us were not only fishing for our own breakfast, but without even bait on the hook. Which all goes to prove that the Americans are a great people, and as shown by the people of the South and its progress that they will get there, bait or no bait, pants or no pants; and it teaches also a lesson to all foreign powers at this late day that even with a small Navy and no fortifications for harbor defense that we would be a bad people to catch even with our "pants down," so to speak.

CHAPTER V

While Lee's army was quiet at Bunker Hill, recruiting in numbers and gaining in bodily strength after the severe campaign of the summer, the powers at Washington were urging McClellan on, to raise cane with Uncle Bob Lee; but they could not get him to go. Lee was not only at Bunker Hill, but he was on his own "dung hill" and he knew it, and knew he would spur, as he had been there before. Finally the Federal Army commenced to slide down toward Fredericksburg in a kind of half-hearted way, altogether too slow for Stanton, and off went the head of McClellan, and that was the end of him. He retired to New Jersey, and became a looker-on.

McClellan went to Europe for a few years. He served a single term as Governor of New Jersey from 1878 to 1881. For Little Mac's version of the events of the war while he was commander, see McClellan's Own Story.*— Ed. 2016*

[Ambrose] Burnside, the man that gave the name to the whiskers [sideburns], was appointed to fill his place. He told these folks at Washington the plain truth: That he could not lick Bob Lee's army; but they would not believe him, and patted him on the back, and told him "to go in;" hurried him forward to Fredericksburg, thinking that he would be there before Lee. It was no go. As usual there was someone there to receive him, deputized by Lee for that purpose, with the usual instructions to give the gentlemen a very warm reception, if he desired to visit the old town, and inform him that he must first get a permit from R. E. Lee.

"It was told that Mr. Lincoln, on being applied to for a pass to go to Richmond, told the applicant that a pass from him would do no good, as he had given to McClellan and about 200,000 men just such a pass to go to Richmond, and that those people down near Richmond either could not read or paid no attention to it, as it had been nearly two years, and they had not got there yet."

In the meantime Lee, with the remainder of his army, was quietly coming southward to assist in the reception to be accorded the visitors at Fredericksburg.

34

That march from Bunker Hill to Culpepper Court-House will be long remembered by the men of the Army of Northern Virginia, or that part of it to which I was attached at that time—R. H. Anderson's division. We were poorly clad, and in my company, out of about 57 men, we had 17 without shoes. (I was orderly-sergeant at that time and made the report as to the number.) It was in November, and very cold for that month, I remember when we forded the Shenandoah River that the ice was one-half inch thick. At Culpepper the shoeless men got shoes. They were made from the green hides of the cattle killed for food, sewed up with thongs or strips cut from the hide, the hair-side being inside, next to the foot. These moccasins, or whatever you may call them, were about 16 inches long, and the beef were on them. The men put them on while green, and in a' few days they dried, and there was no getting them off without cutting them. It was lucky that there were no dogs in camp or they would have given us trouble. We were bad off in the clothing line.

I am fully satisfied that were I to appear on any stage today clad as I was at that time, including those shoes of hide, that I would be a drawing card for the show. (These are facts, not colored.)

We continued our march in a few days to Fredericksburg, and arrived there about the 4th of December, 1862. Soon after our arrival the surrender of Fredericksburg was demanded by Burnside. The request could not be granted just then, and he was quietly so informed.

While Burnside was waiting for his pontoons, Lee was assembling his host on the hills back of the old town, and early in December all were up and waiting the visit of our friends over the river. It was determined by Lee and his generals, with the assistance of his old army, when they did come over to tender them the hospitalities of the State of Virginia in a manner becoming the occasion, and to make that reception as warm as possible. In a few days the demand was again made for the surrender of the town; but he said no; but if it would be any accommodation he would request the people of Fredericksburg to vacate for a short time. Which he did. This was December, cold and bleak.

Reader, do you wonder, when the Southern soldiers saw the women and children tramping from their homes at that inclement season, and camping in the woods without shelter, I say, do you wonder that every soldier in that army made a vow that such treatment should be avenged. Let history tell how fearfully it was kept.

On the morning of December 11, 1862, about 3:80 a m., I was up. I had some early cooking to do. There was but one utensil for that purpose in our company; and one of the boys had the evening before became possessed of some cornmeal and had given me some of it. Under the early-bird rule that got the worm, I concluded that the early soldier would get the skillet, and therefore got his meal cooked first, and I was the only one that got my meal cooked that morning. Just as I had finished cooking it a Whitworth gun from Lee's hill sent a sound forth that intimated to me, as orderly-sergeant, that I had better form my company. I soon had the company astir and in line. That gun told Lee's army that Burnside was crossing the river, and the people of Fredericksburg were to be avenged. Yes; the people of Fredericksburg were to be avenged! and one of the most bloody repulses was to be inflicted on Burnside's troops that had occurred during the war.

I shall merely glance at this battle, giving such statements as I was an eyewitness to, or such as was well authenticated by other persons who saw it in other parts of the field. During the 11th Lee quietly began placing his troops in line of battle. There seemed to be no hurry or confusion. There was a place for all, and the troops were slowly marched to their places.

I remember that our division marched very slowly, and did not get on the line until night. Probably this was done to conceal our movements. I presume it was, as we could have been in position in two hours, if necessary. Burnside made the attempt to lay his pontoons early in the morning of the 11th, but was prevented by the sharpshooters of Barksdale's Mississippians, which so enraged him that he opened his artillery on the town and caused great destruction of property by fire, but very little loss of life. After several hours of this artillery fire he made another attempt to lay his bridges; but the Mississippians were still there. He finally sent, in boats, a large force, and Barksdale fell back by Lee's orders, as the purpose was only to delay Burnside until Lee was ready. It never was the intention of Lee to prevent them from crossing. All day of the 11th and 12th the Federal Army was getting over the river, and Lee was quietly awaiting on the hills his advance.

About 9 o'clock on the morning of the 13th we knew that the battle would soon commence, and one hour later it was in full fury. It happened that my regiment was sent out as a picket line, just to the left of Jackson, and as we were not engaged I had a full view of the Federal lines as they advanced to attack Jackson's lines at Hamilton's Crossing. It was Meade's division that led the advance, and I must say that the troops moved forward in splendid order and stood the fire well. They advanced well up, and it was horrible to see the slaughter. One line would melt away and another take its place to meet the same fate until five lines had been cut to pieces. For about one hour the slaughter went on, and then Meade withdrew near the river. These men had no chance of success from the beginning, and it looked like murder to send them in there. With the falling back of Meade the fighting ceased on this part of the line (the right). I did not see the fighting on the left; but history tells us it was even worse. At Marye's Heights it was bloody. I saw a man coming out from that point. He said that he had looked at the dead until he was sick, and I think he told what was so, as he stated that there was no danger where he was, and he simply was tired of killing men (sharpshooter). There had not been more than one-third of Lee's army engaged, and his losses were small compared to Burnsides, about 2,000, while Burnside's (officially) was 12,000. Thus the people of Fredericksburg ware fearfully avenged.

The people of Washington now believed what Burnside told them: That he could not whip Lee. But it cost them 12,000 killed and wounded to be convinced of what he had said when appointed. Burnside retired across the river, and the powers at Washington soon retired him from command of the army.

Fredericksburg was indeed a terrible disaster for the Union.—Ed. 2016

Lee's army went in winter quarters. Around in this section where we rested for the winter—my division was near Guinea Station on the Richmond and Fredericksburg Railroad—nothing to do to keep my mind employed, I was again struck with the idea that I was a poet, and laboring under that delusion I managed to produce [a] doggerel, which we used to sing to the tune of "Caroline of Edinburgtown." Some of the old people recollect that song, and if they think they can sing I have no objection that they should try. It is copyrighted; but if the words don't kill them and their neighbors, I have no objection to the use of it, provided I am not held liable if any damage should occur:

Thus runs the thoughts of the soldier after a battle—grief for the comrades gone and thanks for a victory gained, and yet both grief and thanks are soon forgotten in his own trials and sufferings.

General Burnside gave us very little trouble the balance of the winter, except making us move out of camp on the 9th of January, to meet what is known as the mud march in history. It did not amount to much, only to put his and our troops to inconvenience and cause a great deal of profane language among the men. While the winter was hard it did not cause Lee's army much suffering. We passed the time in quarters, or holes in the ground, huts, and such other shelter as we could provide.

Two of Longstreet's division (Hood's and Pickett's) were sent to Suffolk after meat early in March, and not only succeeded in getting considerable meat, but drew quite a large number of troops to that point to prevent us from taking possession of Norfolk. I was in Pickett's division at this time, and we had quite a number of men belonging to that section of country, ail near our homes; and here was again tested the manhood of our boys. They had been away from home for a year, and were in a position to leave the army and go home. The temptation was great; yet there were no desertions. Every man did his duty; and when, on the 3d of May, we withdrew from that point, the honor of each man had been tested, and each had proved his manhood. While I was at Suffolk the battle of Chancellorsville was fought. After the failure of Burnside at

38

Fredericksburg his head soon fell in the basket as commander of the army, and "Fighting Joe" Hooker was appointed to the command.

I feared Hooker. I had considered the idea that he would do some damage, and from his manifesto to his army in the latter part of April it looked as though he thought so, too. In so many words he told his army that Lee, including Jackson and Stuart, in fact the whole outfit of the Confederacy, was the lawful property of the Army of the Potomac; and as he was now, about May 1st, ready, he determined not to wait until Hood and Pickett got up from Suffolk, but would go over and take possession of what was in sight.

We know that this was not the first time that such claim of property had been set up. [Union General Irwin] McDowell at the first battle of Bull Run set up just such a claim. On July 21, 1861, and on the 22d, a great many of his men were looking for Beauregard and his animals in the city of New York, without guns to kill or lassoes to tie the animals with.

Lee was a just and honorable man, and as Hooker had claimed him and his army he had no desire to go off and thereby defraud him of his property. So when Hooker started out to fulfill his mission of taking possession of the 50,000 men of Lee, Lee simply placed them so that Joe could get them with the least difficulty.

The battle of Chancellorsville was the outcome of this arrangement of Hooker. We all know that Hooker got his property, but it was too hot and heavy to take over the river when he went back. There were numerous other things which he did not take with him, such as guns, small arms, munitions of war, and he left his dead and wounded, with numbers of real live men as prisoners of war.

The Battle of Chancellorsville is often referred to as Robert E. Lee's "perfect battle." It was another disaster for the Federal forces, and Lincoln was heard to say, "My God! My God! What will the country say?"—Ed. 2016

I shall not go into details of this battle, as I was not there, and what I would say would only be from the knowledge of others. We know that when Joe was safe from harm he told the people of the

North and his men that he and they had done pretty well (I suppose he meant in getting away), and gained quite a victory; but I have never yet found any one that believed that.

While there was great rejoicing at the South for this victory, there was also great sadness for the loss of Jackson, who by his great generalship and success had endeared himself to the entire South; and in fact his name was known throughout the entire world at this time.

From the first Manassas, where he gained the name of Stonewall, in each successive move he had added to his fame new laurels, until that day at Chancellorsville when, with 25,000 men, he was about to place himself in the rear of Hooker, with 90,000, and teach the world new features in warfare; but on the eve of what was to be his greatest achievement, and would have classed him the greatest general of the age. In the twilight of the evening by his own men he fell, and the entire South was filled with grief; but he uttered no word of condemnation on his men. He quietly submitted to the will of that Allwise Providence, and passed from darkness into light. But we missed him on every battlefield from that time to the end; and to-day there is not one high-minded man throughout this entire country that will refuse to pay a just tribute to the memory of Stonewall Jackson.

Even many Union soldiers recognized Jackson's greatness and mourned his loss as an American man.—Ed. 2016

CHAPTER VI

Soon after the battle of Chancellorsville Hood's and Pickett's divisions joined Lee near Culpepper Court-House. The South was in good spirits. Victory had perched on the banners of the Confederacy, and it was determined to again try invasion. The army was being reorganized into three corps—commanded by Longstreet, the right; Hill, center, and Ewell, the left. The army was fairly well clothed and equipped. Just before starting there was a review of all the cavalry and part of the infantry at Culpepper Court-House. There I saw for the first time Belle Boyd, the noted rebel spy. She was not a handsome woman, but might be called dashing; that is, she looked so to me, as I was not in the habit of seeing many women those days.

About the middle of June Ewell's corps started for the Valley. Hooker seemed to know nothing of this move, and lay quietly at Fredericksburg, refitting and organizing his army.

It was wonderful how much killing those Irish and Dutch in the Federal army could stand. But the Federals always managed to get some more men to fill up the places made vacant. There was much bounty in the North and much bounty jumping. In many instances the same fellow was hired several times, and is s ill alive and drawing his pension to-day like a little hero, and to hear him talk you would think he ought to have been killed several times, and, in fact, so he ought, under the rules of war, been hung. It was this class that greatly helped to create the war debt and helps to impoverish the country with the vast pension list. The real soldiers of the North should see to it that all such are dropped from the rolls, if such a thing is possible.

But I am digressing. I said that Hooker was quiet and seemed to know little of Lee's movements, until from the Valley came the astounding news that Winchester had been captured and nearly all of the army of Milroy destroyed. Longstreet was following Ewell northward. Hooker hearing the above news moved from Falmouth and set Hill at liberty to follow Longstreet. Lee must have known his man well to make this audacious move in the face of 100,000 men; that is, stretching his army out over 100 miles, making of it a very thin skirmish line. It can only be accounted for by supposing Hooker to be completely demoralized and feared to approach Lee. There is no wonder; for when a man gets as badly whipped as Hooker was at Chancellorsville it takes him a long time to get over the fright. I don't think Hooker ever did get fully over it, as he soon asked to be relieved. Alter the capture of Winchester Lee moved forward with little difficulty, and nothing of note occurred until the army crossed the Potomac, about the 24th of June, Ewell in advance, Hill and Longstreet well closed us. As we advanced into Maryland, amid the green fields, the spirits of the troops seemed to gain new life. It began to look to them as if they were on their road to plenty, if not peace.

On the 27th Ewell was on his way to Carlisle, and Longstreet and Hill at Chambersburg.

On the 28th Hooker was relieved from the Army of the Potomac and Meade appointed to the command.

General George Gordon Meade was considered by Grant (at the end of the war) one of two generals in the Federal army most suited to large commands, Sherman being the other. Meade wrote to his wife that when he was awakened in the early morning hours of June 28, 1863 by a messenger from President Lincoln, he thought he was going to be arrested. Instead he was given command of the Army of the Potomac just three days before Gettysburg. See The Life and Letters of George Gordon Meade.—Ed. 2016

Meade said but little on taking command. I suppose he knew the story of the poll parrot that did too much talking, and got its neck wrung, and he therefore kept quiet. But there was one thing that he did say that went to show that he was not so sure of the final outcome, and that was to order the immediate shooting of any soldiers who did not stick, therefore placing a fellow between two fires. If he did he'd be shot, and if he did not he'd be shot. He also told his generals to make speeches to the men and tell them the necessity for sticking. Lee never had to issue such orders to his men. There is one other notable think that, although Virginia had suffered the wanton destruction of private property, in some cases virtually by orders of the officers commanding, as in the case of Pope and lesser officers, yet Lee, by his published orders, would not permit any wanton destruction of private property. The contrast was so great that some of the Northern papers commented. But many of the people of Pennsylvania seemed to think that we would eat them. I was amused at a Dutch family near Chambersburg. I, with two of my company, got leave to go out to get cherries. We carried our arms with us by orders. We approached a house. (In that State they bake bread for the week at a time.). The lady was at her baking. I politely asked her if we could get some cherries. Her husband came up, and joined in the conversation. He told me that he had been trying to get a baking of bread for his family, and as fast as he got it done some of the soldiers would come and buy it from him (of course paying for it in Confederate money), and what he had in the oven was the last flour that he had. I said, "Why do you sell it to them?" He intimated that he was afraid to refuse. I told him that he stood in no danger. The next soldier who wanted to buy his bread to tell him the state of affairs and not sell it. With his consent I went up the cherry tree, and while there had the satisfaction of hearing the lady refuse the next buyer, and she was surprised at the gentlemanly manner in which he took the refusal.

It is true that our commissary purchased all of the goods in the different towns; but then they, like any other customer, paid for them in good Confederate notes, and was perfectly willing, if there was any change, to take it in greenbacks, or even gold, or, if they preferred, to give them an order on the United States Government. The seller, as a general thing, doubted the possible acceptance of such orders; but at the close of the war they were of great use to the smart ones who took them as proof of their claim for loss.

Some of the people around that section were equal to bounty jumpers.

Some soldiers enlisted for a $300 bounty. They would then "jump" the enlistment and go to another regiment and enlist for another bounty.— Ed. 2016

It was related to me by a Federal soldier (he had a leg off [i.e., amputated]) that a man living near Gettysburg, after the war, put in a claim for $400 against the Government and a like amount against the State also. This gentleman was sent to investigate it. He found the losses sustained as follows: House used as a hospital by the rebels; parlor wall spattered with blood; keeper off the front door: well-house filled with straw for wounded; the loosing of one calico dress, cost about one dollar; twenty chickens; the whole not exceeding $25. Taking such charges as this in consideration we can readily see how such vast fortunes were made and how the war debt reached up in the thousands of millions.

Ewell was, on the 28th, on his way to Harrisburg, Longstreet at Chambersburg, and Hill near them. Immediately on Meade assuming command of the Army of the Potomac, then at Frederick, Md., he put it in motion for Gettysburg; but his engineers were looking for a line near Pipe Creek. In fact, while he was going forward, he was looking for a place to get back to (history), and I have no doubt that he fully expected to do so.

At that time Lee was without his cavalry, and his information was not as reliable as it should have been. Receiving the intelligence that Meade was moving on Gettysburg Lee knew that his communications would be endangered, and therefore ordered Ewell back from Harrisburg to Gettysburg, and put Hill in motion for the same place; also two of Longstreet's divisions; Hood's and McLaw's were ordered to Gettysburg; Pickett's remaining at Chambersburg as a rear guard of the army. Thus we find, the last day of June, both armies approaching Gettysburg. Destiny had pointed out the path. They were following it.

I shall describe what I saw of this battle and what I learned of it from men who were on different parts of the line, and were reliable, with more minuteness than I have other battles, because it is conceded that this was the turning point of the war. On the last day of June, or rather the morning of July the 1st, Gettysburg was virtually surrounded by nearly 200,000 men of both armies, varying in distance from 8 to 30 miles.

The old world is dotted with historical points and numerous battle fields that are famous. This continent, or the United States, had just commenced to make its historic spots. Virginia had nearly all of note up to this time; but now Gettysburg, with its diverging roads, was about to become the most famous town and spot on this continent. It was an inland and obscure town, but by the decree of fate the curtain of obscurity was withdrawn, and Gettysburg, Pa., was to become, on this 1st day of July, 1868, known throughout the civilized world. Two armies, composed of American soldiers, were about to meet in deadly conflict. Two armies, such as this continent had never seen before, commanded by the ablest soldiers of the age, and each fighting for what they conscientiously believed to be holy, right, and just. The soldiery qualities of the American people were to be tested to their full extent, and on these beautiful fields, amid the hills, where nature seemed to have expended vast labor to beautify. Soon they were to be turned into a pandemonium, and amid the rattle and roar, smoke and fire, the passions of men and his powers of destruction were to be witnessed.

On the 1st day of July, 1868, Hill's Confederate troops were in motion, advancing toward Gettysburg, on the Chambersburg pike. Buford's cavalry was also in motion, moving through Gettysburg. About two miles west of the town they met, both officers deployed their troops, and the dropping fire of small arms told that the battle had begun. Soon General [John] Reynolds came up with part of his first corps Each side was being reinforced, and General Buford gathered up his cavalry and retired to the rear, so as the infantry might have a chance. Thus at about 10 o'clock the battle was growing strong. The Federals were pressing on as though they meant fight, and Hill's advance was getting the worst of it. Soon General Reynolds was killed. [General Oliver Otis] Howard was soon on the field. His eleventh corps was coming into line on the night of the first, and at nearly right-angles with it, and covering Gettysburg to the north. Hill was being pressed, but was holding on well, bringing forward his troops as fast as he could; but soon this would change. About 1 o'clock, from the north, one of Ewell's divisions were seen in the distance approaching. He soon had his artillery in position, and its thunder was added to increase the storm of battle. Soon the second division came up, taking places on the left of Rhodes, he extending to the right, and about 3 o'clock he found an opening in the Federal lines between the two Federal corps. Rhodes was a good soldier. He did not hesitate, but hurled his men into the opening, and the fight for that day was won. The right of one and the left of the other corps of Howard was driven back. Hill was relieved of the pressure. Early advanced on the left and Hill on the right, thus completing the victory, and in a few minutes the Federal troops were in full retreat through the town of Gettysburg, and being pressed by the Confederates. The loss of Hill was severe; but we were fully compensated for it. The 1st and 11th corps were nearly ground up. They left 5,000 prisoners in our hands, besides their killed and wounded.

Thus ended the first day. The battle closed at 5 o'clock. Why was it? Let history answer. To say that Hill's and Ewell's troops fought with their usual gallantry would be useless at this time. The world has long since admitted that the soldiers in the army of the Confederate States were the equal of any soldiers of the world, and it takes but few words to express their qualities—bravest of the brave. Of course I am prejudiced; yet I have the world at large as my authority.

The first day at Gettysburg was only a prelude of what was to follow. During the night both armies were being hurried forward by their commanders. Meade had determined, at the suggestion of Hancock, to make his stand here, and wisely. Nature had made this locality for a field of battle, if nature does such things. The position held by Meade was one of the best for defense that could have possibly been found in this locality; and during the night to the natural strength Meade was adding artificial works, and by 12 o'clock, July the 2d, it was almost impregnable to any other but Lee, and to any army but his it would have looked that way. But Lee knew his army, and knew that if such a thing was possible at his command they would accomplish it. And being placed in such a condition that he must cripple his adversary before retreating, if it should become necessary, Lee determined to make the attempt to carry Meade's lines by assault. To that end he commenced to make preparation, and ordered Longstreet to assault Meade's left and Ewell to advance on his right.

The Army of Northern Virginia and the Army of the Potomac had often before met amid the smoke of battle and clash of arms; but this day, July 2, 1863, was destined to surpass in blood and death all former struggles. Men were on this day to grapple in the agonies of death and fall side by side and expire.

At 4 o'clock in the evening Longstreet was ready. Opposite were the lines of Meade, bristling with steel, sullenly awaiting the onset, not knowing when or where the blow would fall; but it soon developed. Longstreet gave the command, and at his word 100 guns belched forth their smoke and flame, and sent out howling, shrieking, crashing across the field their iron messengers of death. The wager of battle was accepted by Meade, and the answering thunder of his guns added more confusion to the storm of battle. This infernal din and destruction was kept up for more than half an hour, and then was seen to move forward the veterans of Longstreet. Steadily they advanced across the field. The crash of musketry joined the roar of artillery, and amid smoke and fire these men moved steadily forward. Sickel's [sic] troops had been thrown forward, and they were the first to receive the shock.

Union General Dan Sickles had thrown his troops out to the Emmitsburg Road without orders to do so. This left the Union left flank hanging.—Ed. 2016

Bravely they held their ground for a time; but Longstreet's men fought with a desperation that could not be resisted, and gradually Sickle's was being forced back by McLaw's men. Inch by inch, foot by foot, the ground was given. The fight was terrible. Breast to breast men fought, fell, and died. Suddenly we see Hood, with his Texans, press forward to the right of McLaw and envelope Sickle's left, and his line gave way. The tide of battle was in favor of the men in grey. Hood, sweeping to the right, sees that the key of the position is Little Round Top. He immediately placed himself in front of his men and ordered them forward to that point. Then the rush for victory commenced. Up that steep and rocky ascent those men of Hood went. Hearing the top they met the fire of musketry in their faces, and then commenced a struggle for the mastery like the world had never seen before. With bayonet thrusts, firing in each other's faces at three yards, dying together, and falling down the mountain side as they died. This bloody work went on until the mountain side was red with blood. But the end was coming. Hood's men were being decimated by shot and shell—outnumbered. Finally they fell back, amid a shower of musket balls, to the low ground. Sickles was still being pressed back by McLaw's, and this continued for more than a mile. For three hours this hell on earth was kept up until night put an end to it. The losses on both sides had been severe, and Longstreet had accomplished nothing to recompense him for it. After night the grey lines fell back near their old position, and thus ended one of the most bloody and persistent attacks of the war. On the right (Meade's) Ewell's success had been better. He had charged with his division up the rocky steep of Culp's Hill and penetrated the Federal lines, and at night held them. Thus the 2d day of this modern battle closed. The valor of the troops had been tested to their fullest extent, and in no case found wanting. But the bravest troops in the world cannot accomplish impossibilities.

It is useless to mention regiments and brigades. Suffice it to say to that these men were of the Confederate army.

At night, July 2d, the men were resting on their arms, worn-out with the day's fighting, and thinking of comrades who had fought their last fight. Thousands of homes, both North and South, would be filled with sorrow for the husband, father, or brother who would never come again.

The silent stars looked down on the faces of the dead and blushed for the passions of men. The wounded were being cared for as well as possible under the circumstances, and the living were thinking of the morrow. Thus passed the night.

July 3, 1863, dawned, and all was activity. Both commanders were astir early and in council with their subordinates. This day, perhaps, would determine the success or failure of one of these armies. Meade during the night had straightened his lines and was in a better condition than the day before. Lee viewed his lines, looking for the place that might show some signs of weakness, but found none he had tried both wings, and now, after due reflection, determined to strike the center of Meade's army, and if he could break through and reach the Baltimore pike, then good bye to Meade's army, and his head would fall in the basket. Thus we find the situation on the morning of July 3, 1863. This day was to become one of the days memorable in history. Yet the quiet that prevailed in the early morning gave no signs that within the radius of 10 miles were concentrated nearly 150,000 soldiers, and that two days' fighting had taken place in the vicinity. Yet such had been the case, and at that time every house and barn within miles around were filled with the wounded of the two armies.

Soldiers know little of what is taking place outside of their immediate commands. They hear the roar of artillery and crash of battle, and see the wounded coming from the front and hear all kind of rumors and reports, and there their knowledge ends.

Lee having determined to make the attack the orders were given to Longstreet, and he began to make ready for the attack. Pickett's division of Virginia troops, to which I belonged, had arrived on the evening before. (I shall tell this from actual knowledge.) We had moved from Chambersburg in the early morning of the 2d, an I marching 27 miles halted, and went into camp about 4 miles in rear of the line of battle. We knew that a severe battle was going on in front, and we also knew that there had been a fight on July 1st, and that our army had been very successful.

Although the roar of artillery was sharp at the front and the wounded were being taken to the rear, we of Pickett's division were tired and hungry, and paid attention to the part of hunger at once. After eating and resting a short time we were ready to hear the news of the day.

Of course rumors of all kinds reached us. It was finally known to us that, while the battle was somewhat in our favor, that it was not decisive. As early as 9 o'clock that night we knew that our services would be required in the morning, but were in hopes that it was for pursuit only, as our division was the reserve of the army.

As early as 3 o'clock on the morning of the 3d of July the division was stirring and under arms, ready to move forward. We little dreamed what was before us on that memorable day. We moved slowly forward, and about 10 o'clock we took position on the line of battle, facing Meade's left center and on the right of Hill's division and slightly in advance. It soon became known that our (Pickett's) division was to attack (luring the day. It had been slightly hazy, with fleeting clouds, but the sun had come out in all its brightness, and it was extremely hot and oppressive on the men, many of them in the open field. As the day progressed it became a certainty that we were on the eve of something desperate, and finally each regiment was informed what it had to do and what was expected of it.

Up to this time, near 1 o'clock, all had been quiet; artillery had been moving into line and taking position; but there was not even an occasional shot to disturb the quiet. About I o'clock the sound of two Whitworth guns broke the stillness, and immediately 125 guns, all along the line, joined in. In a few moments the Federals opened with about 80 guns and joined in the infernal din that fairly shook the mountains. The smoke soon darkened the sun, and the scene produced was similar to a gigantic thunderstorm, the screeching of shot and shell producing the sound of the whistling blast of winds. Man seldom ever sees or hears the like of this but once in a lifetime; and those that saw and heard this infernal crash and witnessed the havoc made by the shrieking, howling missiles of death as they plowed the earth and tore the trees will never forget it. It seemed that death was in every foot of space, and safety was only in flight; but none of the men did that. To know the tension of mind under a fire like that, it must be experienced; it cannot be told in words. There is nothing to which I could compare it so as it would be made plain to one who had never been there. For two long hours this pandemonium was kept up, and then, as suddenly as it commenced, it ceased. For a few moments all was quiet again. Then was to come the work of death. (I was a member of Armistead's Brigade.) The command attention was heard, and the men rose from the ground, where they had been lying during the fire of artillery.

If I should live for a hundred years I shall never forget that moment or the command as given by General Louis A. Armistead on that day. He was an old army officer, and was possessed of a very loud voice, which could be heard by the whole brigade, being near my regiment. He gave the command, in words, as follows: "Attention, second battalion! battalion of direction forward; guides center; march!' I never see at any time a battalion of soldiers but what it recalls those words. He turned, placed himself about twenty paces in front of his brigade, and took the lead. His place was in the rear, properly. After moving he placed his hat on the point of his sword, and held it above his head, in front of him. Much has been written of this charge, and it has become historical.

It is not egotism in me to be partial, because I was a soldier in it. For this charge and the gallantry shown by this division on that occasion is not only the property and glory of its men, not only the glory and pride of Virginia, but it belongs with all its glory to the entire people of the South as much so as do the deeds of the Confederate armies.

Therefore I am simply trying to describe this onset of Pickett's division with a truth and accuracy as I saw it and as I recollect it, and will try not to exaggerate the action of the division or cast reflection on others.

In a battle like Gettysburg, when all did their duty, when men faced death with seemingly no fear; when nearly every State in the South was represented, and today have to mourn the loss of hundreds of their sons, whose bodies sleep beneath the soil of Pennsylvania in unmarked but honored graves. When these same sons, in life as one grand whole, made up the Army of Northern Virginia, commanded by that great and noble man, Robert E. Lee, I say that the acts of every regiment, brigade, and division, of every officer and soldier, added glory to that army. That it was the property of all, and all should cast aside any feeling or thought that would tend to cloud the title of any to an equal share in the glorious deeds of that army, which the world has admitted to have been one of the greatest, in all respects, of modern times. With this explanation of my position I shall proceed.

I said that this charge had become historical, and yet little has been said of the gallant Armistead; therefore I must devote some few words to him. With his hat on his sword he led his brigade, being in front of it, and cheering it on. His men saw him. They saw his example. They caught his fire and determination, and then and there they resolved to follow that heroic leader until the enemy's bullets stopped them. It was his example, his coolness, his courage that led that brigade over that field of blood, through a fire of shot and shell, that the world had scarcely ever witnessed before, and the survivors of that brigade wherever met will testify to his gallantry and their love and respect for his memory.

The division moved forward at command, in common time, and as it cleared the woods its work was seen before it. Long lines of bristling bayonets and the blackened mouth of numerous artillery, which at the time were quietly awaiting to deal death and destruction to us. But the men in that line, by their steady step and well-dressed lines, seemed to be determined to do or die.

(The writer of this was a second lieutenant and file-closer at that time; that is, in rear of his company, and could see all that was in front.)

All was quiet; we had cleared the woods, and advanced about 200 yards. (We had about one mile to go before reaching the Federal lines.) Suddenly about fifty pieces of artillery opened on our lines. The crash of shell and solid shot, as they came howling and whistling through the lines, seemed to make no impression on the men. There was not a waver; but all was as steady as if on parade. Forward was the command, and steady, boys, came from the officers, as we advanced. Crash after crash came the shot and shell. Great gaps were being made in the lines, only to be closed up; and the same steady, move-forward; the division was being decimated. Its line was shortening, but as steady as ever, the gallant Armistead still in the lead, his hat working down to the hilt of his sword, the point having gone through it. He seemed to be as cool as if on drill, with not a sound of cannon near. We were nearing the Emmitsburg road. There were two fences at that road, but they were no impediment. The men go over them, and reform and forward again. At this point the crash of musketry was added to the roar of artillery. Men were falling in heaps. Up to this time no shot had been fired by this division.

Within 300 yards of the Federal works Garnett's brigade give their usual yell and strike the double-quick. At 100 yards they deliver their fire and dash at the works with the bayonet.

Kemper's brigade takes up the yell, fire, and dashes at them with the bayonet. Armistead, who is a little to the left and rear, catches the enthusiasm, joins the yell, and, on the run, Armistead fell back to the rear to give his brigade a chance to fire. They fire and rush at the works and to the assistance of Garnett and Kemper. There are shouts, fire, smoke, clashing of arras. Death is holding high carnival. Pickett has carried the line. Garnett and Kemper are both down. Armistead dashes through the line and, mounting the wall of stone, commanding "Follow me," advances fifty paces within the Federal lines, and is shot down. The few that followed him and had not been killed fall back over the wall, and the fight goes on. Death lurks in every foot of space. Men fall in heaps, still fighting, bleeding, dying. The remnant of the division, with scarce any officers, look back over the field for the assistance that should have been there; but there are no troops in sight; they had vanished from the field, and Pickett's division, or what is left of it, is fighting the whole Federal center alone.

We see ourselves being surrounded. The fire is already from both flanks and front; but yet they fight on and die. This cannot last. The end must come and soon there is no help at hand. All the officers are down, with few exceptions, either killed or wounded. Soon a few of the remnant of the division started to the rear, followed by shot, shell, and musket-balls.

Out of 4,800 men in line that morning there was not more than 600 left to tell the tale of our annihilation. Fully sixty per cent were dead or wounded and the balance in the hands of the enemy. This ended the battle of Gettysburg.

Lee expected a Union counteroffensive and tried to rally his center, telling returning soldiers that the failure was "all my fault." Pickett was inconsolable. When Lee told Pickett to rally his division for the defense, Pickett allegedly replied, "General Lee, I have no division!" Pickett's report of the battle has never been found.—Ed. 2016

The climax of hard fighting was over. Begun by Hill and Ewell on the first day, continued by Longstreet on the second day, and closed by Pickett on the third day.

At 5 o'clock that evening Lee was at bay, and woe to the troops that dared to advance against him. His old army was there, just as defiant, just as full of fight as ever; and Meade knew it, and took the wise precaution of not attacking.

On the night of July 3d, over on Seminary Ridge, stood the old veterans of Longstreet, Hill, and Ewell just as defiant as ever. They had seen their comrades on the past three days give their lives freely as they had often seen other comrades do before. They knew that they had met with a bloody repulse and great loss; but they knew that Lee was still there and they were ready to obey his command and follow where he ordered. Their confidence in him was not the least shaken, nor would it be even to the end.

While the Army of Northern Virginia was for the time checked, it had shown to the world of what stuff it was made; and in the three days' fighting it had shown to the world a gallantry that would go down the ages and grow in brightness as time rolls on.

Meade by his action in not moving forward admitted its greatness. He knew that it was intact and could not be demoralized; and when that fact, under the circumstances, was admitted by an enemy, there is no reason why we should not be proud of the old heroes. They stood defiant for two days, awaiting attack, and then at Lee's command moved back to Virginia, checked, but not a defeated army.

Here I leave you, grand old army, loved Lee, and comrades of my sufferings. A new life is before me. I had passed over that field of fire and death. I had followed Armistead until I saw him fall. I had walked back over the wall, and being the only officer at that point, I assumed command. The men fought with desperation, cool and courageous, until surrounded on all sides. I finally gave orders to all to look out for themselves and my duties ceased as an officer from that time. Believing it my duty to remain at that wall as long as there was any hope, I remained until the question was whether I would die or be captured. I chose the latter, and found myself a prisoner of war. In passing to the rear of Meade's army I saw that which, if it had been known to Lee, even then the battle might have changed. In fact at that point Meade's army was whipped. Worse, it was demoralized, and to a large extent; but this knowledge was of no value. I could not communicate it to headquarters.

Though Meade was criticized for not pursuing Lee immediately, the twin Union victories of Gettysburg and Vicksburg, one day apart, gave the Army of the Potomac and the North a great boost in morale.—Ed. 2016

CHAPTER VII

Virtually I was dead as far as my services to the Confederacy was concerned. Classed among the missing in the report of my company; but I turned up within the Federal lines, alive and well in body, but not in mind. The surrounding circumstances were strange, and created a feeling that I recollect at the time was unexplainable. The word dazed about expresses it. But in a few hours I began to realize the situation. I was in a camp with about 1,800 others, from all parts of our army. The Yanks had seemingly made a haul. At 9 o'clock that night the provost-marshal-general made a speech to us. Among other things he said "that General Longstreet was captured and various other generals killed or captured. In fact that Lee's army was gone up," and wound up by saying "that we were surrounded by several hundred guards, and at the first attempt to escape he would open fire and slaughter us indiscriminately."

July the 4th we were taken to Baltimore. Rough marching and some brutality among the guards toward the prisoners. For a few days we remained at Fort McHenry, and where then sent to Fort Delaware. At that point the officers were separated from the privates and sent to Johnsons Island, Ohio, in Lake Erie.

I did not have much time to see prison life at Fort Delaware. The trip to Ohio took three days. We were fed at Pittsburg. Arriving at the island, in Lake Erie, at sundown our names, rank, etc., were taken, and we were committed for the offense of being in rebellion, and at times were to enjoy about the same treatment that was accorded to American prisoners on the prison ships by England in 1876.

All have read or heard of the reported treatment of Federal prisoners at Belle Isle, Libby, and Andersonville. Such might have been the case. It might have been true but there was some excuse for it. The Confederacy could not feed their armies. It was impossible to care for the suffering population near these prisons; but in the wealthy North with its fields teeming with grain, amid plenty, it may perhaps sound harsh, but it is a fact when I say that men suffered, yes, starved, at Johnsons Island, Ohio. At this late day it is not necessary to call up recollections only for the truth of history. This state of affairs as regards prisoners of war was brought about by ignoring the cartel of exchange. We know that the South had nothing to do with that, as we were always ready to deliver prisoner for prisoner, and toward the latter part of 64 we were willing to send North men even without men in exchange. Therefore the blame must fall on Stanton, who was Secretary of War. And from my standpoint as a Confederate prisoner, and I believe from the standpoint of Federal prisoners, that we were justified in visiting the severest condemnation on him while living, and to try and forget, now that he is dead, that he ever lived.

On our arrival at Johnsons Island, we were informed by the prisoners there before us that the ladies of Sandusky, Ohio, which was just across the lake, gave a party, with wine, cake, and their presence, to any soldier who shot a rebel, and that we would have to be very careful or we would pay the price of a party. I don't know about the party part, but I do know that several prisoners were shot on slight provocation, but the men who shot them had never been to the front, or it would not have been so. Life in all the prisons of the North was about the same—one of misery, suffering, and many deaths. It is not perhaps generally known, but it is a fact that there were more deaths in Northern than in Southern (statistics say so) prisons.

It is true that there were times when men forgot their Sorrows, and life was endurable. We had men of all classes in the different prisons, (I visited forcibly Point Lookout, Fort Delaware, and Johnsons Island). Store keepers, manufacturers of bone trinkets, jewelry, in fact most anything, could be bought, provided a man had the money. We had some amusements—singing, preaching, debating clubs, etc. I was a washer woman; I did washing and ironing, and by them made my tobacco; for be it known that we had millionaires in prison, men with money.

After returning home in '65 I suggested to my wife that I could help her iron the clothes; she let me try, and decided that I was not a Chinaman in that respect; but I managed to make the rebels at the Island think so.

57

One evening, after my washing was done, sadly thinking of what was and what "might have been" that Great Delusion of mine got the upper hand of my judgment, and I again imagined that I was born a poet.

Nearly every day there would be rumors of the renewal of the cartel of exchange, but it never came; we all know at this time, and knew then, that it would not do to give Lee anymore men; the Federals could get all they wanted, and could afford to let their men die in Southern prisons, and help to eat up what little food we had. "Oh, Stanton, how is it with your soul."

Time passed by, and this life in prison was almost unendurable. Numerous schemes were tried to escape; one or two attempts on a large scale were started, but failed; finally in January, '65, the exchange was commenced, but very slowly, so slowly that only a few got through before the close of the war. I was on my way to Richmond when it fell, and was sent to Fort Delaware, and was kept there until June 13, 1865. It was a question with us what was to be our fate; it was said that all of the officers were to go to the Dry Tortugas, and it did begin to look that way, but on the 13th of June, I, with about 300 others, was released, given transportation, and told to go and sin no more. I arrived home on the 15th, to find my wife on the verge of the grave. My little children did not know me, and wondered what right I had there, but as their mother made no objection I remained, and I have been there ever since. Those little boys and that little girl are now married, and I have numerous grandchildren. My wife suffered all that it was possible for a woman to suffer and live. I found her health broken, with eyes impaired from constant sewing to keep bread for her children. We are now growing old, and looking back and remembering all of our trials, the friends that are gone, we can say that both of us were honest in our opinions. "That we believed then that we were right and that we believe now that we were right then."

FINIS

Made in the USA
Middletown, DE
15 September 2018